# HIDDEN TREASURES

## STAFFORD

Edited by Allison Dowse

First published in Great Britain in 2002 by
*YOUNG WRITERS*
Remus House,
Coltsfoot Drive,
Peterborough, PE2 9JX
Telephone  (01733) 890066

HB ISBN 0 75433 882 7
SB ISBN 0 75433 883 5

# FOREWORD

This year, the Young Writers' Hidden Treasures competition proudly presents a showcase of the best poetic talent from over 72,000 up-and-coming writers nationwide.

Young Writers was established in 1991 and we are still successful, even in today's technologically-led world, in promoting and encouraging the reading and writing of poetry.

The thought, effort, imagination and hard work put into each poem impressed us all, and once again, the task of selecting poems was a difficult one, but nevertheless, an enjoyable experience.

We hope you are as pleased as we are with the final selection and that you and your family continue to be entertained with *Hidden Treasures Stafford* for many years to come.

# CONTENTS

# The Poems

## IN A FAIRY STORY

In a fairy story
The world can be
As red as a fire breathing dragon
As orange as sparks spurting from a wizard's wand
As yellow as the princess's silky, long hair
As green as the wicked witch's face
As blue as a sea monster roaming the deep
As dark as a black knight's castle
As black as a witch's cat
As bright as a brave knight's armour, shining in the sun.

*Daisy Cuffley (9)*
*Brooklands School*

# A STORMY NIGHT

When the night draws in
And the wind starts to shriek and moan
The ducks and swans swim away
When the trees creak and groan.

The clouds are turning black and blue
And the insects have been and fled
Thunder and lightning fills the sky
While children are tucked up in bed.

We all dash in
Away from the wet
Out of the cold and into the warm
Away from the wind, the rain and the storm.

*Lucy Brands  (10)*
*Brooklands School*

## LITTLE FOALS

Lovely little foals, as sweet as can be
Taking their very first step.

Lovely little foals, all different colours
Tasting their very first drink.

Lovely little foals, legs as long as their mother's
Taking their first look at the outside world.

Lovely little foals, I remember one well
Now she's three years old.

*Lydia Paris  (10)*
*Brooklands School*

## AT THE CIRCUS

At the circus the world can be
As red as a clown's squeaky nose
As yellow as salted buttered popcorn
As blue as the seal's nose ball
As green as the face of the tightrope walker before his first step
As orange as the flame-thrower's fire
As purple as the late night sky
As pink as the laughing children's faces
As dark as the stallion galloping loudly around the ring
As bright as the sequins on the trapeze artist's costume
As white as the ringmaster's shirt
As black as the panther obeying commands
As silver as the chains keeping the tiger at bay
As gold as the money taken by the cashier.

*Sophie Kenny (9)*
*Brooklands School*

# DEEP IN THE WATER

Deep in the water
The world can be
As red as coral swishing
As orange as a crab walking by
As yellow as the sun at the top of the ocean
As green as the seaweed floating by
As blue as a whale swimming past
As dark as the rock's shadow
As black as an eel wriggling past
As bright as a shark's teeth gleaming.

*Joseph Cowling  (10)*
*Brooklands School*

# SUN

A sun is like a light bulb shining in the sky
Waiting till it has been blown out in the midnight sky
It is like a frog jumping from lily pad to lily pad
When it rises above the morning clouds.

*James Morgan  (11)*
*Brooklands School*

## MY BOOMERANG

My boomerang is an orange banana
Flying through the air.
It goes round the lamp post
Like a paper bag in the wind.
It turns like a bird,
Coming crashing helplessly to the ground.
I pick it up and fling it through the air;
It spins like a plane out of control.
Then it slows down like a car coming to traffic lights.
It is now an orange banana skin,
Sitting in a world of its own
Waiting for me . . .

*Caroline Saxon  (10)*
*Brooklands School*

# THE PLANETS

The planets are enormous coloured spheres floating high in space
Planets are like gas giants with their anger building up
Into raging storms
The moons revolve around the planets like spinning tops
On a black table
The planets are giant apples with an enormous central core
Eventually the core will be penetrated by the erosion of time
Far out in space the planets are like balls on a black snooker table
The white surface of the moon reflects the light at night
Like gigantic torches shining towards the Earth.

*Sami Qureshi  (10)*
*Brooklands School*

# A STAR

Twinkling away
Like a diamond floating in the night sky
Talking with others
As it sails by
Sometimes shooting
Like a bullet from a gun
Working hard with fellow stars
Making patterns in the sky
A shining tear deep in space
Giving light to the world.

*Alex Roberts  (11)*
*Brooklands School*

# THE WIND

The wind, when stormy is like a giant's breath
It is a huge hairdryer that has not been switched off
The wind is like a giant's fist knocking down the walls of houses
It is a bomb leaving behind a trail of mass destruction
When all is calm the wind is a small child breathing softly
Or a fan cooling someone down in the summer sun.

*Alex Horwath  (11)*
*Brooklands School*

## THE SEA

The sea is an orange soda as the sun sets
As it drains down my mouth like the tide going out
Like the tide going out to sea
The orange soda is forgotten
Until the morning rush
People trying to get into the sea
On a hot summer's day
There is a queue in the shopping market
People trying to get the lovely drink
At the end of the day
It is left to carry on the everlasting cycle
On and on in the morn.

*Luke Paterson  (10)*
*Brooklands School*

# CATS

Cats are little children
Sitting in the corner
Playing with little teddies
When they get home they just want to sleep
They love being fussed like unwell children.

*Hannah Beard (11)*
*Brooklands School*

## THE PEN

Like a snail leaving a trail of ink,
On its way to the other side of the page.
A pen is filled with red blood,
Losing more and more as it writes.
Later on he is put into a pencil case,
With his brothers and sisters,
Like a lipstick being put into a purse.

*Eve Cotterill  (11)*
*Brooklands School*

# THE DUSTBIN

Sitting innocently on the pavement
Like a drunken tramp on the sidewalk
The dustbin tumbles
Cymbals are crashing
As a shabby cat scavenges for food
The bin is abandoned on the floor
Like a forgotten drunkard
Asleep outside *The Swan*.

*Matthew Pratt  (11)*
*Brooklands School*

## THE BLACK HOLE

The black hole is the swirling grave of a star
As it travels
Through no-man's-land
Like an oily vortex
Light years away
Alone
Alone
Alone.

*Paul Greaves (11)*
*Brooklands School*

# THE HARBOUR POEM

Guides showing people to their boats
Lifeboats ready to rescue
Sailors in danger
The sea calm and cold
Ships going out to sea
People going to the shop to buy fishing tackle
People fishing all day
The catch of the day
Coming off fishing boats at the quay.

*Christopher Holland  (10)*
*Brooklands School*

# THE MARKET

The market's full of busy people,
The market's full of happy people,
The market's full of chatty people,
The market's full of rushing people.

The market with stalls full of fruit,
The market with stalls full of clothes,
The market with stalls full of sweets,
The market with stalls full of plates.

The market where the tramps come to beg,
The market where the old lady sells her cakes,
The market where the butcher sells his chops,
The market where the farmer sells his eggs.

Come to the market on Monday or Sunday,
Come to the market in rain or in sun,
Come to the market on your own or with friends,
Come to the market with lots or with little money.

*Our market is great!*

**Jack McCann (10)**
**Brooklands School**

# MOON

The moon is like a football
Lost and never found by its owner
Or a boomerang
That has failed to return to whoever threw it
A ten pence piece flipped into the air
To decide who starts in a 5-aside football match.

The moon is a dinner plate
On a dark blue table cloth
Or a piece of cauliflower
On a dark blue plate
The moon is an unhappy sun
Too sad to shine.

***Benjamin Hughes (11)***
***Brooklands School***

# A CHIMNEY

C himneys are as tall as giants
H eaving out smoke like an aeroplane's plume
I nside is as dark as the night sky
M any have tops like a queen's crown
N ew ones are like daisies
E very old one is covered with black soot
Y elling out pollution.

*Sarah Marshall  (11)*
*Brooklands School*

## KITCHEN COLOURS

Deep in the kitchen
The world can be . . .
As red as a juicy tomato
As green as a crispy and wet lettuce
As orange as the satsumas in the fruit bowl
As yellow as ripe bananas
As blue as the water running from the tap
As purple as the African violets growing in a pot
As pink as my mum's apron as she cooks tea
As black as the Aga warming your hands on a cold winter's day.

*Edwina Mellor  (10)*
*Brooklands School*

## MORNING IN THE COUNTRYSIDE

Cows munching the green fresh grass of the morning
Birds singing their songs
Field mice run through the corn
To escape the starving cat
Farmers in their tractors starting their daily chores
Country lanes noisy with cars and cyclists.

*Alex Freshwater  (11)*
*Brooklands School*

## DEADLY TEACHERS

Yes, unfortunately I have a deadly teacher,
It's definite, she's a talking creature!

No matter what I say or do,
She always says, 'I want a word with you!'

You don't know what they'll come up with,
In fact, you should be surprised I'm allowed to live.

Oh why do we have deadly teachers? Life is so unfair,
Hang on, can this be true? There's a nice one over there!

*Zoë Dudek (10)*
*Cooper Perry Primary School*

## THE MANKEY PEPPER!

Yuck! Yuck! Mankey! Mankey!
It looks like someone's snotty hanky
Red, green, yellow or worse
If you eat it you might need a nurse
If you feel sick leave the room
Or else prepare to meet your doom
The mankey pepper really reeks
It makes tears roll down your cheek!

*Kelly Greaves  (11)*
*Cooper Perry Primary School*

# FEET

Feet are smelly like an old welly
Feet are big like a fat pig
Feet are hot like kitchen pots
Feet are mucky, all black and sooty
Feet are wet with sticky sweat.

*Laura Newton  (11)*
*Cooper Perry Primary School*

# MURDER IN THE KITCHEN

I looked down at the table
The knife gripped tightly in my hand
My stomach gave a horrible lurch
As I prepared to complete my mission.

I raised the knife high in the air
And brought it down making a huge
*Thud!*

I opened my eyes and tears slowly fell
I had done it and as I looked down
It was there, cut in half - the onion.

***Amy Millward  (10)***
***Cooper Perry Primary School***

## MY HORSE

I have a horse
I have a lovely horse
She eats her hay
Down at the bay.

She likes me to ride her
So I call her Piper
She runs like the wind
And follows my mind.

When she's in her field
She goes all wild
When she's in her stable
She's sleeping like a child.

*Emma Wilson  (10)*
*Cooper Perry Primary School*

# SCHOOL DINNERS

That green mush they slop on your plate
Looks like someone's already ate
As for that grey-brown hash
On that you don't want to waste your cash.

The dinner ladies prowl the room
Get away from them - zoom, zoom, zoom
So if you really want something to munch
Take my advice, bring your own lunch!

*Grace Howden (10)*
*Cooper Perry Primary School*

## HIDDEN TREASURE

It's precious gold, I can't believe it
A blast of sticky honey which tickles your nose
Shining, glittering, dazzling, amazing
It's been shipwrecked, stranded on a little beach of its own
Still giving off its beam of magical, sparkly light
An old, jolly man finds it, his face lights up like a bulb
The treasure starts to gleam again, and is given a new life
With a loving, caring person to help its eternal spark.

*Chloe Dennis (9)*
*Cooper Perry Primary School*

# HIDDEN TREASURE

Taste rich like sticky honey
Hard and rusty just like money
Glitters in a tart
Looks like daffodils and attaches to your heart
Up the chimney, down the cellar
And everywhere you go you will get richer and richer
Sparkles, glitters, shines like a star
Dropped in a jar
Dropped down a drain
Everywhere you go you will drop it and drop it
You find it in a cave
You save it in a bank
You find it under the sea
And it vanishes off your knee
You find it underground
Then you realised it was a pound.

*Matthew Gill  (10)*
*Cooper Perry Primary School*

## SCHOOL DINNERS

You sit down at school dinners,
Look at the lumpy gravy,
And throw up under the table,
Don't even try getting away,
You will get extra custard,
And believe me, you don't want the custard
The dinner lady shouts out, 'Seconds!'
*Zoom!* Everybody's out of the room!

*Jason Littlewood  (10)*
*Cooper Perry Primary School*

## THE MOULDY OLDIE PEPPER!

Err! Err!
What's that over there?
Is it a tomato or is it an orange,
What could it be?
I know what it is, it's a mouldy oldie pepper.
The pepper is horrible,
It looks like a dustbin lid
And smells like a load of rotten eggs.
It just sits there ready for the smelly bin,
I would not eat the mouldy oldie pepper,
I would rather eat boiling hot lava.

*Stacey Robinson  (11)*
*Cooper Perry Primary School*

# HIDDEN TREASURE

It's hidden somewhere
Under the sea
I hope I find it
Before it finds me
I have found it
It's here with me
It has been all along
It's hidden treasure
In the heart of me.

*George Foxley (9)*
*Cooper Perry Primary School*

## CHILD'S DREAM

Maximum quantity of happiness,
Unlimited loyal friendships.
Hidden worlds, magical creatures galore,
Lands of gold, lands of jewels.
Crispy ice on a winter's morn,
While the robin chirps cheerfully.
Dreams from which no one wants to be woken,
Dreaded places where terrible things lurk.
But where there is hope the worlds still go on.

*Robert Newman  (9)*
*Cooper Perry Primary School*

## HIDDEN TREASURE

It's gold, sparkling, smooth gold
It's diamonds, glass, sparkling diamonds
It's jewels, flames, red, orange.

*Giles Baugh (9)*
*Cooper Perry Primary School*

# HIDDEN TREASURES

Hidden treasures
Oh, this will be a pleasure
It may be found
But it may be bound in a box.

If I find it, I will be glad
But this may be bad
Gold, silver, rubies or crowns
Or it just may be a million pounds!

*William Bott (10)*
*Cooper Perry Primary School*

## MY SPECIAL THING

My special thing sits on my bed
He's a teddy bear, I call him Ted

He sits right there, all alone
Waiting for me to come home

He's big and round and rather fat
He's almost bigger than my cat

I have had him years and years
He's lost all the fur behind his ears

He's got a little button nose
He likes to have a little doze

I feel sorry for him sitting there
But he's my special teddy bear.

*Becky Cock  (11)*
*Cooper Perry Primary School*

## KITTEN!

Paws of silk
Loves her milk
Claws of steel
Slices her meal.

Catching mice
Not very nice
Pulling voles
From down their holes.

You'll never believe it
She'll never even eat it
She'll only play with it
Then do away with it!

But all of the time
She's really cute
And as soft as a mitten
Yes, that's my kitten!

*Richard Hie  (11)*
*Cooper Perry Primary School*

## GOLDEN TREASURE

It's gold, sparkling gold
Sparkling, shiny, dazzling and exquisite
It's been shipwrecked, washed up on the shore
Rich, enchanting, precious and spellbinding
Its taste is like hot toffee bubbling in your mouth
Astonishing, glorious, glistening and happiness
It sparkles and glitters in your eyes
Exciting, shiny, gleaming and magical . . .

*Leah Francis  (9)*
*Cooper Perry Primary School*

## HIDDEN TREASURE

Treasure isn't all it seems, it's sticky honey from bumblebees
I sit down below the sea, waiting for someone to rescue me
Then I am stranded on a beach with fighting pirates hunting for me
Oh no! I'm captured, off we go, off to England, here we go
Then I am displayed in a posh museum, everyone wants to see inside
But all there is is an empty heart waiting for someone to fill it with joy
Then I see her, here she comes with her bright blue eyes
And her dazzling heart
Here I go, I'll hop inside
Then my treasure is my *heart!*

*Jessica Hughes  (9)*
*Cooper Perry Primary School*

# IN THE PLAYGROUND

In the playground
At the back of our house
There have been some changes

They said
The climbing frame's not safe
So they sawed it down

They said
The paddling pool's not safe
So they drained it dry

They said
The see-saw's not safe
So they took it away

They said
The sandpit is not safe
So they fenced it in

They said
The playground's not safe
So they locked it up

Sawn down
Drained dry
Taken away
Fenced in
Locked up

How do you feel?
Safe.

*Michael Peacock  (9)*
*Cooper Perry Primary School*

## HIDDEN TREASURE

You can find treasure on islands
Also on shipwrecks and underground
Always danger lies ahead
You can find treasure where it's hard to get.

*Matthew Atkin  (9)*
*Cooper Perry Primary School*

## MY FAMILY TREE

My family is my treasure, as I couldn't do without them,
My Auntie Lorrie helps me piles,
My Uncle Roger is funny and makes me laugh,
My grandma and grandad spoil me heaps,
My cousins are friendly and funny,
My nana is precious and pampers me loads,
My mum is a darling and always there,
My dad is a sweetheart when he's in the right mood!
And then there's me.
My Auntie Dorothy was lovely, I miss her a lot,
My poppa was helpful and handy, but now he's gone,
My cousin Guy was really matey, but he's departed us too,
And then there's me.
Stuck in the middle with all this going on,
Being sensible and enjoying myself!

*Jessica Smith  (10)*
*Cooper Perry Primary School*

## HIDDEN TREASURE

It's hidden down below our depths
In a load of wooden junk
Where pirate ships have sunk
Someone's heart will lead them to it
And others will just have a fit
People sink down below trying to reach me
But they all fail
Pirates get their ship and crew and bravely set sail.

*Harriet Trussler  (10)*
*Cooper Perry Primary School*

## HIDDEN TREASURE

Sparkly, gleaming gold,
Amazing, dazzling, magnificent, shiny,
Old and ancient but very magical,
Tastes like sticky, glorious honey,
Shipwrecked on an island,
Rich, precious, enchanting, exquisite,
Hard, astonishing, charming to see,
Glitters everywhere,
Jewels, sparkling jewels.

*Aimee Rawsthorne  (10)*
*Cooper Perry Primary School*

## MY HIDDEN TREASURES

Is it under the sea?
Is it under the floorboards?
Mine is in my heart
My treasures are my grandads
They're always in my heart
Even if I only knew one
I will always love them both
The grandad that I knew
Was as tough as old boots
But as loving as a puppy
And as sweet as honey
Well
My other grandad . . .

*Francesca Pennicott  (10)*
*Cooper Perry Primary School*

## ARE YOU HIDING HONEY?

Buzzy, buzzy, busy bee
Is going off to find his tea
Sticky, gooey, oozy honey
To them just like money
Over the wall smelling the smells
Leaving all those honey cells
Out in the open far and wide
Leaves tickling by its side
Smells of hedges with round red berries, yum!
Oh, he loves thinking about that in his tum!
Sticky, oozy, gooey, lovely, smelly, oozy honey
Past the hawthorns prick, prick, prick!
Evil things they lick, lick, lick
Down the winding, twirling bench
Almost there now, teeth are clenched!
Over here, it's a weed
Oh no! That's all he needs
Here we are at last a rose
Sniff around with his nose
At last that honey
Oh, it's just as rich as money
Glorious feeling, silky glow
Mixture of chocolate dough
So sweet to get that thing inside
All those wonderful things combined!

*Emily Parker (10)*
*Cooper Perry Primary School*

## MY HAMSTER

My hamster is called Whitey,
He is very strong and mighty.
He always goes in his wheel,
To have a three course meal.
He gets out of his cage,
Then he goes on a rampage.
Throws his cage on the floor,
He gets stressed even more.
That's my hamster for you,
I've got to go, see you.

*Oliver McGregor  (11)*
*Cooper Perry Primary School*

## SCHOOL DINNERS

School dinners aren't bad
As for the dinner ladies
They're mad
If you like their lumpy gravy
Then you've got to be crazy!
Take my advice
If you have their curry
You'll need the loo in a hurry
If that doesn't turn your belly
Wait till you hear
About the ice cream jelly
I think it's about time
I ended this rhyme.

*Oliver Wall  (11)*
*Cooper Perry Primary School*

# MY FAT PETS

My fat dog
Is as hard as leather
And hates going
Out in rainy weather.

My fat cat
Think about that!
It sleeps all day
Then parties the night away.

My fat mice
Like to eat rice
They're oriental too
And like to nibble at my shoe.

*Patrick Holden  (11)*
*Cooper Perry Primary School*

## BATS

Bats are the best
Flying around all night
Eating mice all night
Playing around with the other bats
Scaring you at night!

*James Dalton  (9)*
*Doxey Primary School*

## THE CHEESY MOON

The moon looks like white cheese,
I like cheese but I don't like peas.
I want to be an astronaut,
But have to go through scary training.
First go down a twirling slide
Into a deep pool of water,
Then get thrown into a thing
That goes different speeds.
Fast, slow, at last it stopped,
I came out flat as a pancake,
The training was finished.

*Dayle Archer  (10)*
*Doxey Primary School*

## BOOKS

Books are boring
Books are fab
Books have pictures
Some have none!

Goldilocks is gold
Red Riding Hood is red
But what colour is Rapunzel?
She's got ripples in the water.

Books are boring
Books are fab
Is there anything else
Except books!

*Tania Simpson-Wood (10)*
*Doxey Primary School*

## WAR AND PEACE

War was vicious
Full of terrible deaths
Tanks, planes and infantry
All fought to save other people
I wish one day the world
Would live in *peace!*

**Sam Ford  (10)**
**Doxey Primary School**

# DAYDREAMING

Here I am daydreaming
In Mr Wood's class
I dream I'm picking flowers
From the newborn baby grass.

Here I am daydreaming
Wishing to be a pop star
Touring in America
And travelling very far.

Here I am daydreaming
Wishing to shop at the mall
Now I'm on the beach
Playing volleyball.

*Cherisse Samantha Jones  (11)*
*Doxey Primary School*

## DAYDREAM

I'm walking in football wonderland
Every day people cheering
Driving my Porsche
Signing autographs.

I'm so happy when I'm playing
Scoring a hat-trick
I go to the crowd when they're chanting
England, England, England.

Craig, Craig!
Huh!
What's nine times nine?

*Craig Lorne  (11)*
*Doxey Primary School*

## WEIRD RHYMES

I can see
A mouse scurrying
A mother giving her child a clout
My sister hiding
My best friend a-riding
But what is weird?
My dad was feared
And a grandad growing a beard
A boy drinking Diet Coke
And a girl having a stroke . . .

*Rachel Eve Milgate  (10)*
*Doxey Primary School*

## THREE LITTLE SPECKLED FROGS

Three little speckled frogs
Sat on a tree log
Eating little bugs - yum, yum
A frog ate all the bugs
And ended up at the bottom of a great big lake.

Two little speckled frogs
Sat on a tree log
Looking for tiny bugs - yum, yum
One frog fell in a hole
Landed on a metal pole, oh no!

One little speckled frog
Sat on a tree log
Sitting all alone
Suddenly lightning struck
And blew him up
Oh no!

No little speckled frogs
Sat on any logs!

*Edward Painter  (10)*
*Doxey Primary School*

## DREAMS

Dreams, dreams, dreams
How I love to dream
Sitting in my bed
And it hurts when I bump my head.

Dreams, dreams, dreams
How I love to dream
Sitting in my chair
Cuddling my teddy bear.

Dreams, dreams, dreams
How I love to dream
Sitting at the table
Reading a fable.

*Jemma Clews  (10)*
*Doxey Primary School*

## DREAM TIME

Dreams, dreams, dreams
That's all they seem
Beautiful colours
That's all they mean.

Dreams, dreams, dreams
In my head
Then I wake up
And my memory's dead.

Dream time, sleepy time
Sleepy time, sleepy time
When I count sheep
I fall asleep.

Dream time.

*Annabel Pattyson (10)*
*Doxey Primary School*

## DREAM TIME

Dream time, shut your eyes, go to sleep and dream
I dream about my dancing
Before my mum comes in and wakes me up.

Look at all these people sitting in these chairs
I hear someone calling my name
Oh no, I've won the Britz award.

Why am I at the seaside
Playing with Britney Spears?
Pinch me, somebody pinch me!
So I know that this is not true
I think I like all this dreaming
So Mum, please don't wake me up.

*Hayley Flint  (11)*
*Doxey Primary School*

## DREAM TIME

Fire, fire you're so bright
Sometimes you are a fright
You heat up the whole house and make it a bright light
Fire, fire you're so sparkly and sharp
Fire, fire you're so flarey, you make my skin hairy
Fire, fire you always flicker and bicker
Fire, fire you're so bright
That's what I dream all night.

*Tom Waines  (10)*
*Doxey Primary School*

## DREAM TIME

Dream time, dream time
Rushing through the sky
Crying in my head
Flying under my bed
Leaving sweet dreams
All through my head.

Up into space, down into towns
I realise how my favourite dream
Has been found.

*John Lyons  (10)*
*Doxey Primary School*

## DAYDREAM

D ream, dream, I dream about Man Utd winning the cup
A ll day Man Utd are still celebrating
Y ears have gone past, a new season starts
D reaming of winning the cup again
R eds are playing Liverpool, Man Utd won 2-1
E riksson cheering when the champions win
A ston Villa we are playing next
M atch ends, 6-0 to the Reds, that means we have won the cup again.

*Caroline Gascoyne (10)*
*Doxey Primary School*

## MY KITTEN

My kitten's cute and soft
She comes when I call her for dinner
She gulps it down *fast!*

*Nadine Cooper  (9)*
*Doxey Primary School*

# THE SOLAR SYSTEM

Mercury's the closest one
The closest to the shining sun
Venus is so hot you'll boil
Poisonous gases rising with great toil
Earth is like the shape of a peach
It takes the sun's light eight minutes to reach
Mars is the colour of bright red
With its storms you'll never get to bed
Jupiter is made of gas
Letting lots of satellites pass
Saturn with its beautiful rings
It floats in space but it doesn't have wings
Uranus is the one that's green
A million years or more it's been
Neptune is not very warm
It has lots of nasty storms
Pluto is the furthest one
The furthest from the shining sun
Now we're into deep, dark space
We've left the sun's great shining face.

*Thomas Belcher  (10)*
*Doxey Primary School*

## WHAT AM I?

I live in a tree
I am three inches tall and I am very fast
But no, I'm not a bird
I can't fly
What am I?

I live in the North Pole
I blend in with the snow
I am very big
I like to eat fish
What am I?

I live in the jungle
I have a long mane
Some people say I'm ferocious
What am I?

I live in your home
I am smaller than you
I like to go on walks with you
What am I?

*Reanne Barnes-Davies  (9)*
*Doxey Primary School*

## SCHOOL DINNERS

Ding, ding, ding
The bell goes ring
Dinner time, get in line
5, 6, 7, 8
The line must be straight
Dinner, off you go
Chop-chop, you don't want to be too slow
Off you go.

Sausages, bacon, egg and chips
Yum-yum, we lick our lips
Drink, this is tricky
Yes, it's going to be this milky.

Look at this bacon
It's all green
And the milk's all red
It's like jam on bread
Yuck, yuck, yuck.

The egg is all runny
That's not really yummy
The chips look like brown led
No, it might be green or red
I hope tomorrow will be better
Tomorrow I'll choose better.

*Jade Wood  (10)*
*Doxey Primary School*

## UP IN SPACE

Up in space
Where everything is so dark
Behind the moon
Where aliens lark, up even higher
Where gravitational limits are far
It wouldn't even weigh down a hundred pound car
All different gases filling the air
Like stars twinkling
Don't have a care.

*Ashton Moores  (10)*
*Doxey Primary School*

# MIRROR, MIRROR ON THE WALL

Mirror, mirror on the wall
Who's the bravest of them all?
You are the bravest of them all
Mirror, mirror on the wall
Who's the prettiest of them all?
You are the prettiest of them all.

Mirror, mirror on the wall
Who's the ugliest of them all?
Your sister is the ugliest of them all
Mirror, mirror on the wall
Who's the dumbest of them all
Your sister is the dumbest of them all.

Mirror, mirror on the wall
Who's the bravest of them all?
You are the bravest of them all
Mirror, mirror on the wall
Who's the prettiest of them all?
You are the prettiest of them all.

Mirror, mirror on the wall
Who's the ugliest of them all?
Your brother is the ugliest of them all
Mirror, mirror on the wall
Who's the dumbest of them all
Your brother is the dumbest of them all.

*Damen Richardson  (9)*
*Doxey Primary School*

## MY DOG SKIP

In the morning
My dog Skip
Will wake up
From a long kip
Shortly after he plays with my old sock
When I feed him
He nips my hand
It does not hurt
But I love him so much!

*Jonathan Cooke  (10)*
*Doxey Primary School*

## ON THE RUN

Bang, bang, bang
The British fire
The tanks and infantry are brave
Fighting in the desert
Private, corporal, lieutenant, major too
Fighting hand in hand
Saying this is for valour
We will die in honour
Most know they will perish for their country
But they still fight on
Heads held high, chins all up
Some say we will win and never lose
If they fight together
Finally they do win the war
Get the Germans on the run
They did it for King and country!

*Sam Turner (9)*
*Doxey Primary School*

# CHRISTOPHER

My brother is sixteen
He smells horrible
He is very bald
He never takes a bath
He never stays at home
He is very tall
He is very greedy
He is always taking food
Out of the cupboards
His room is sometimes messy
He is very scruffy
He is always playing on the PlayStation
Sometimes when he is doing his homework
He puts the radio on full blast
And my mum tells him to turn it down
He tells me to get out of this room
Sometimes we play on the computer
We take it in turns
I quite like my brother.

*Daniel Woo  (7)*
*St Bede's School, Wolseley Bridge*

# MY ROOM

My room is a dump
Smelly socks in the corner
A big black TV on a chest of drawers
Clothes on the floor
Boxes full of toys in the wardrobe
Juggling balls on the bed
A box of chocolates behind the door
Chocolate wrappers in the bin
Wallpaper with elephants and giraffes on
I hate my bedroom
I've had it for eight years
If I could get another bedroom
I would feel better
For the next eight years.

*Eliot Byrne  (8)*
*St Bede's School, Wolseley Bridge*

# MY DAD

My dad is cool
He doesn't shout at me
He buys me presents
When I want to have a walk
We go on a walk
My dad is brilliant
Sometimes he buys me lots of sweets
He bought me a little TV and some toys
I read with my dad
He fixes people's teeth
He likes to go fishing and tie flies
Sometimes I catch a trout with him
My dad is excellent!

*Michael Neary  (8)*
*St Bede's School, Wolseley Bridge*

# MY DAD

My dad's cool
He takes me to the park
He cleans up for me
When I've eaten my dinner
He always buys me Lego
Every morning he cooks me a sausage butty
His fringe is in an 'M' shape
He goes to squash loads of times
Because he's got nothing to do
He takes us to see Wolves play
When they're playing at home
He wears lots of sports clothes
And he goes to the gym
He used to play for Tottenham and Millwall
My dad's really great.

*Paul Rose  (8)*
*St Bede's School, Wolseley Bridge*

## MY FAIRY

My fairy has long, golden hair
Not as nice as my yellow chair
You must never touch a fairy, don't you dare!

My fairy has red, red lips
As red as a rose
The finest you've ever seen.

Her shoes are made from pollen
So pretty and so pure
Her wings are very clear
You can never be so sure.

You must see how they fly
So high up in the sky
The fairies are so small
You can't see them much at all.

Their shawls are made of light petals
The softest you shall feel
Their wings are rainbow colours
The fairies are very real!

*Grace Coggins  (8)*
*St John's Catholic Primary School, Great Haywood*

## EASTER

E   is for the Easter eggs in a little box
A   is for the afternoon when we eat them all
S   is for the shining sun on the golden wrapper
T   is for the toffee in my crunchy mouth
E   is for the Easter bunny hopping around all night
R   is for the rainbow when his work is done.

*Alice Norbury (9)*
*St John's Catholic Primary School, Great Haywood*

## CHOCOLATE CAKE

Chocolate cake, chocolate cake,
The scrummy, yummy chocolate cake,
The layer of butter cream inside,
Oh it definitely does not hide.

Chocolate cake, chocolate cake,
The icky, sticky chocolate cake.
Don't forget the chocolate top,
Oh there's loads more than a lot.

*Elizabeth Adams  (9)*
*St John's Catholic Primary School, Great Haywood*

## WINTER

Winter brings the snowflakes
Which flutter down like butterflies.

Children make some snowmen,
Smart and well behaved,
They never make a sound.

*Alicia Smura  (9)*
*St John's Catholic Primary School, Great Haywood*

# A CHRISTMAS POEM

Bells are ringing in the street,
Baubles hanging from the trees,
Children playing in the white crisp snow,
Bare branches on the trees,
Swaying in the gentle breeze.

Log fires burning in the warm, cosy houses,
Homes full of joy and happiness
As they carve the turkey,
Then it's time for Christmas cake,
Yippee!

*Naomi Umerah  (8)*
*St John's Catholic Primary School, Great Haywood*

## MY FAMILY

My family are very silly,
Nearly as silly as a joke book,
Lucy, Mum, John and Dad,
Don't know how to cook!

Lucy's very dumb,
Very dumb indeed,
She'll take the dog for a walk,
And it'll be the dog holding the lead!

John can be so clumsy,
He dropped his mum's vase,
He went to the jungle to get some animals,
And the elephants jumped on the neighbours' cars!

Mum and Dad are very bossy,
They'll smack you on the bum,
If you stuck your tongue out
You could pretend you hadn't done it! Hum! Hum!

*Rebecca Coggins (8)*
*St John's Catholic Primary School, Great Haywood*

## A WITCH'S LAB

Entering the house, going in, looking around,
What do I see?
A witch's broom flying around.

I can hear the witch crackling around,
Oh it's an awful sound.

Saying stop it just won't do it.

I shout and shout till I see something.
Something moves behind the door,
Walking closer, opening the door,
There is a witch, laughing and laughing,
Looking with glee,
Walking closer to me.

*Mitchell Simpkin (9)*
*St John's Catholic Primary School, Great Haywood*

# COUNT DRACULA

Count Dracula is scary,
He'll bite you on the neck.
Although he is a monster,
It's the teeth which are the scariest.

Count Dracula is painful,
He gives you a sharp look.
He lives in Transylvania,
His teeth are shaped like a hook.

The fangs are made to pierce,
To come round every man,
To make two holes at the side of your neck,
He'll bite you if he can.

He hides inside his castle,
He has a siesta in the day.
He comes out at night to give you a fright,
And to scare human spirits away.

*Thomas Tracey  (8)*
*St John's Catholic Primary School, Great Haywood*

## MY GRANDMA

My grandma lives in Birmingham
But she's not a Brummie,
She is very clever,
But also very funny.

She goes to a computer class,
But can't use e-mail.
She's got a brand new car
But she drives like a snail.

She flies around the world
In many different planes,
I often wonder if my gran
Will come back down to Earth again.

*Adam Phillips (8)*
*St John's Catholic Primary School, Great Haywood*

## My Gran

Grannies think they know it all,
They always talk of things they did,
Like in the war.
She goes on and on
About things in the war,
She talks for six hours or more.

*Declan Heath  (9)*
*St John's Catholic Primary School, Great Haywood*

## SEA TREASURE

Pirates floating on the sea,
Just having a cup of tea,
Looking down they see deep below
Gold and silver coins in a chest,
Swimming like a fish down they go.

Pirates collecting coins in their vest,
Pirates swim up to get fresh air.
Back down they go until the coins
Are no longer there.

Pirates rich on their ships,
Thinking of salty fish and chips.
Pirates come back to land,
Dropping coins on the sand,
*Hidden treasure.*

**Alec Ovens  (8)**
**St John's Catholic Primary School, Great Haywood**

## SPAIN

It is our journey to go off to Spain,
although the date has not been set.
But when it has, our car will be loaded,
because we are not flying in a Jumbo Jet.
The journey will be long, over water and land,
but will be worthwhile when our feet touch the sand.

The house is built but the neighbours are unknown,
We can't wait to get in our new home.
The sandy beach is minutes away
where me and my friends will go off to play.

My holidays will be now back to the village once a year,
with this in mind, all the friends we leave behind brings a tear.

*Jak Smith  (7)*
*St John's Catholic Primary School, Great Haywood*

## IN THE NIGHT

In the night things go bump!
They make you go jump!
They bob up and down in our wildest dreams,
But they are not real,
They will always be there.

*Adam Tomkins  (9)*
*St John's Catholic Primary School, Great Haywood*

## THE SLITHERING SNAKES

The snakes slither,
But sometimes they shiver in fear.
They hiss like a kettle sizzling,
Sometimes they rattle their tail like a motorbike,
And sometimes we say yikes.

*Louis Jarrett  (7)*
*St John's Catholic Primary School, Great Haywood*

## MY TED

My special ted
Lives at the bottom of my bed.
He rolls around,
I nearly kicked him to the ground.

I got him when I was three,
That was the day I hurt my knee.

I take him everywhere,
He just likes to stand and stare.

I even take him to the sea where it's very sunny.
My teddy is very fluffy and cuddly.

*Vicky Wills  (8)*
*St John's Catholic Primary School, Great Haywood*

## WINTER

W inter is my favourite season,
I love it best of all.
N ovember we have fireworks,
T hen snow begins to fall,
E veryone moans how cold they are,
R emember to wrap up warm.

*Sophie Greene (7)*
*St John's Catholic Primary School, Great Haywood*

## My Dad

My dad is a machinery dealer,
He drives an eighteen wheeler.
He knows the M6 like the back of his hand,
And we own four acres of land.

We make hay every year
And now the fields are clear,
But it brings money in
Which goes in a tin,
This pays for us to go away on our holiday.

*Rebecca Gregory (9)*
*St John's Catholic Primary School, Great Haywood*

## CALENDAR POEM

January - new beginning as the church bells are ringing.
February - chocolate hearts, the day people come together.
March - the buds are coming out, children are beginning to shout.
April fools, laughs and jokes, the showers on the windowpane.
May - lambs bounding around, making a soft, playful sound.
June - summer sun, school is nearly out.
July - the beach is for me, coconuts in a tree.
August - people getting ready for school to come again.
September - school brings not so many happy things.
October brings Hallowe'en, as the darkness is in a gleam.
November - bangs, crackles and pops, as the bonfire attracts lots.
December brings lots of joy, as you have a Christmas toy.

*Eve Easthope (9)*
*St John's Catholic Primary School, Great Haywood*

# FLOWERS, FLOWERS, FLOWERS

Flowers, flowers,
Lovely flowers,
Flowers tall,
Flowers small,
Flowers blue,
Flowers true.

Flowers, flowers,
Fantastic flowers,
Flowers new,
Flowers old,
Flowers are all different,
That's why I like flowers.

*Nicola Phillips  (8)*
*St John's Catholic Primary School, Great Haywood*

# A Chitanra

It's faster than a cheetah in the jungle chasing a turkey,
Scarier than a monster with yellow eyes and bad breath,
More dangerous than a hissing cobra breathing fire,
Stronger than a giant working out at the gym.

*Ben Lewis (8)*
*Woodseaves CE Primary School*

## THE GRIZDAV

A grizdav is taller than the Twin Towers.
Is heavier than an elephant with pigs on top.
Faster than a cheetah with a jet pack on.
Scarier than hungry lions and bears together.
Stronger than a gorilla, able to bend a human's body
Into a skipping rope.
Fatter than my mother after eating everything in England.

*Timothy Buckless  (8)*
*Woodseaves CE Primary School*

## DOGGIN

A doggin
Is fiercer than a lion catching his dinner,
Quieter than a mouse whispering in assembly,
Faster than a cheetah on roller skates.

Is louder than a lion roaring with toothache,
Furrier than a swinging monkey wearing a woolly jumper,
More dangerous than a tiger in a fight.

Is heavier than a leopard holding weights,
Hungrier than a giraffe on a diet,
More noisy than a snake hissing in a cave.

A doggin has more eyes than a monster wearing glasses,
More frightening than a shark with a broken fin,
Higher than a chimpanzee swinging from tree to tree.

Is stronger than a gorilla going to the gym,
More thin than a bony skeleton in a grave,
Bigger than an elephant standing on my school.

*Katie Faux (9)*
*Woodseaves CE Primary School*

## PEGA SAURUS

A pega saurus is faster than a jet plane shooting in the sky.
A pega saurus is stronger than a dragon wrestling with an elephant.
A pega saurus has teeth sharper than a knife,
Quieter than a mouse crawling on the floor.
A pega saurus is heavier than a ton of bricks.
A pega saurus is taller than the clouds,
Wider than the town hall.
A pega saurus is meaner than a T-rex.

*Rebecca Fox  (8)*
*Woodseaves CE Primary School*

# A STIGERPATHINAKOS

A stigerpathinakos is faster than a cheetah in grass,
Louder than one million trombones playing in a parade,
Fiercer than a fire breathing dragon with a cough,
Angrier than a lion who has a thorn in his paw,
As hungry as a greedy gorilla, who hasn't eaten for a week.

*Jonathan Radcliffe  (8)*
*Woodseaves CE Primary School*

# A GIANT WATER HOG

A giant water hog
Is hotter than a desert in the sun,
Hairier than a monkey who needs a haircut,
Browner than an autumn tree.

A giant water hog
Is fatter than an elephant who is greedy,
Noisier than a monkey being chased,
Taller than a windmill on a high cliff.

A giant water hog
Is stronger than a gorilla who has been weightlifting at the gym,
Faster than a cheetah chasing its prey,
Scarier than a rat and the size of a house.

A giant water hog
Is quieter than a leaf falling from the sky,
Hungrier than a croc on a diet,
Happier than a birthday person opening their presents.

*Rebecka Riley (9)*
*Woodseaves CE Primary School*

## TOZZLING

A tozzling
Is lighter than a feather from a chick,
Faster than a cheetah chasing its prey,
Fiercer than a sharp-pawed, dark pink alien.

A tozzling
Is louder than an angry bear with a headache,
Greener than a crocodile feeling sick,
Happier than a birthday person with the presents he wanted.

A tozzling
Is colder than a freezer in the Antarctic,
Thinner than a pig on a diet,
Braver than a brave jungle hunter.

A tozzling
Is higher than a gorilla swinging from a high branch,
Heavier than a greedy elephant,
Stronger than the world's strongest man.

A tozzling
Is scarier than a blackboard that could talk,
Juicier than a very juicy orange,
As hungry as my mum starting a diet.

A tozzling
Is younger than a day old baby,
Taller than a church steeple standing on a giraffe's head,
More groovy than a posh, groovy chick.

*Becky White  (9)*
*Woodseaves CE Primary School*

## A TIGERFLY

A tigerfly
Is faster than a leopard on a skateboard,
Louder than an elephant stamping in boats,
More beautiful than a princess in her diamond tiara.

A tigerfly
Is quieter than a snowflake falling through the sky,
His teeth are more silver than stars and more sparkly,
Angrier than a lion who has toothache.

*Abigail Anslow  (8)*
*Woodseaves CE Primary School*

## CLINGER

A clinger is a creature faster than a sonic,
Fiercer than a hunting dragon,
Quieter than an ant tiptoeing,
Claws sharper than a cactus needle.

*Howard Kelly (8)*
*Woodseaves CE Primary School*

## GAGASAURUS

A gagasaurus
Is louder than a dragon in pain,
Faster than a zooming car,
Hairier than a woolly mammoth
Who hasn't had his hair cut.

A gagasaurus
Is noisier than a stegasaurus
Who's had his teeth pulled out,
Fiercer than a crocodile
Who hasn't had his tea.

A gagasaurus
Is more colourful than a rainbow,
Taller than a giraffe on tiptoes,
Stronger than a herd of elephants
Who have been to the gym.

*Becky Fowell (7)*
*Woodseaves CE Primary School*

# A BINGLE

A bingle is grumpier than a crocodile with toothache,
Bigger than a giraffe the size of a house,
Faster than a rabbit on a treadmill,
More scary than a snake with a bellyache,
Hairier than a mammoth with a woolly coat on,
With longer arms than the biggest octopus in the ocean,
Noisier than a screeching peacock who's stood on a nail.

*Laura Cliff (7)*
*Woodseaves CE Primary School*

## ZAGREB

A zagreb
Is fiercer than a dragon breathing fire,
Faster than a shark swimming in the dark sea,
Lighter than a monkey in the trees.

A zagreb
Is louder than a crocodile snapping for tea,
More friendly than a mum being kind,
More dangerous than a cheetah chasing a rabbit.

A zagreb
Is scarier than a rat the size of a house,
As hungry as my mum after a diet.

A zagreb
Is madder than a lion who has a toothache,
Longer than a bus taking me to school,
Funnier than my best friend Gemma.

A zagreb
Is stripier than a tiger lying in the sun,
Colder than a polar bear jumping up and down,
Furrier than fluffy slippers.

*Natasha Loewendahl  (7)*
*Woodseaves CE Primary School*

## A Stunk

A stunk
Is bigger than a crocodile on stilts,
Stripier than a zebra with a stripy hairdo,
Grumpier than a dragon running into a tree,
More fierce than a shark who has not had any food.

*Watch out, he's after you!*

**Fiona Jones  (7)**
**Woodseaves CE Primary School**

## BEN

My dog Ben is my best friend,
He will be with me till the end.
Black Ninja is his nickname,
Try to catch him, then he'll go insane.

He's fluffy, furry and clever,
When you wash and brush him he looks as soft as a feather.
He's my dog Ben and he's my best friend,
He will be with me till the end.

*Josie Williams  (10)*
*Woodseaves CE Primary School*

## ANIMALS OF THE WORLD

I could be a tiger, prowling around all day,
Orange, black and stripy.
African or Siberian,
I'm still a tiger with gleaming eyes.
A frog, I would not be
Because it's weak and has not got magical powers.
Maybe I'd be a crocodile
Living in the Nile,
Taking a bath for a while.
A monstrous beast,
To have a big feast,
That's what I would be,
To have lots for tea,
These are the animals created,
Animals, animals, animals!

*Cassie Degg (10)*
*Woodseaves CE Primary School*

## HORSES

Standing in the stable,
Once there was food, now an empty table.
The weight on my back,
It's like a potato-filled sack.
As I am brushed
I eat my oats that are crushed.
Then back to my stall,
Where I stand proud and tall.

I am so beautiful, people gaze
As I chomp and chew and graze.
My hooves are polished and shiny,
I stare at the Shetlands so tiny.
As I gallop through the wood
My hooves get covered in mud,
My coat glistens,
My ears twitch to listen.

My eyes shine and glint
As I crunch my peppermint.
I drink from my bucket of water,
My kick as strong as mortar.
Going to a show,
Over jumps high, but first low.
I stand proud
Listening to the shout of the crowd.

*Rosie Cooper  (10)*
*Woodseaves CE Primary School*

## ANIMALS

Animals pass by through the world looking bright
As we pass in the sunlight.
The animals eat my iced bun,
The baby lambs have lots of fun.
It is fun when dogs chase their tail.
There are lots of animals who live in the zoo
And in the jungle.

*Geraldine Lowndes  (9)*
*Woodseaves CE Primary School*

# DOGS

Brown dogs,
Black dogs,
White dogs,
Spotty dogs,
Daft dogs,
Dopey dogs,
Dirty dogs,
Woof dogs,
Bark dogs,
Loud dogs,
Guide dogs,
Cute dogs,
Cuddly dogs,
Best of all,
I like hot dogs.

*Debbie Talbot (9)*
*Woodseaves CE Primary School*

## APES

My favourite animals are apes,
They love to eat grapes,
Every time I see an ape
I go wild, my mum says I am an ape,
I know all the species,
There are silverback gorillas,
Monkeys and chimps.

My favourite animals are apes,
Chimpanzees in the trees
Crying out for their mates,
One looks like Chris Tate,
Arguing over the women
While the children go swimming,
Orang-utans play in the sun,
I go to the zoo and they pinch my bun.

My favourite animals are apes,
They love to eat grapes,
They sleep under the moon,
They'll wake up soon,
Throwing lemons at each other,
Getting sleepy,
Crawling back to their nest,
Apes are the best.
Waiting for their mum and dad
Who won't be mad.
Picking nits,
Patiently the kids sit
Under, over and up a tree,
Being stung by a bee.
My favourite animals are apes.

*Kirsty Evans  (11)*
*Woodseaves CE Primary School*

## FISH

Flip, flap like my back.
I have a cat on my back.
I get tickled on my back.
I am black.
My name is Jack.
All my family are black.
I sit on the mat waiting for food.

*Martin Cliff (11)*
*Woodseaves CE Primary School*

## ANIMALS

A  nts are small and quick,
N  o one can catch them.
I   n America there are poisonous snakes.
M  onkeys are funny.
A  n elephant is big and smelly.
L  izards are multicoloured.
S  nakes are slimy.

*Eric Kelly  (11)*
*Woodseaves CE Primary School*

## MONKEY

I have a friend called Monkey,
He swings from a tree.
He eats bananas,
He teases llamas.
His eyes are very blue,
He drinks out the loo.
He's my friend,
He sometimes drives me round the bend.
He likes songs,
He smells and pongs
Because he never has a bath.
He makes me laugh,
He tickles me
When I'm having my tea.
Once I took him to school,
He made me look a fool.
He's my friend,
He'll be with me to the end.

*Matthew Atkins  (11)*
*Woodseaves CE Primary School*

## DOGS

Brown dogs,
White dogs,
Black dogs
And ginger dogs,
Fluffy dogs,
Spiky dogs,
And smooth dogs too,
I like any dogs, how about you?

*Joshua Brough (10)*
*Woodseaves CE Primary School*

## I AM LATE

Go faster, go faster,
Pedal, pedal.
I need to go faster, I need to go faster.
Excuse me, excuse me,
I need to get to work,
I need to get to work.
I am late, I am late.
Phew, I am here,
Sorry I am late.

*Alice Shaw (10)*
*Woodseaves CE Primary School*

## DOGS

I like dogs,
They are fluffy and cute.
There are ginger dogs, black and white dogs,
Brown dogs, funny dogs, stupid dogs, super dogs.
I like daft dogs
But best of all is my dog.

*Matthew Burslem (9)*
*Woodseaves CE Primary School*

# CAT, BAT, RAT

Once I saw a cat,
Then I saw a bat,
It flew past,
And fell to the floor fast.

A rat came past,
I heard a blast,
Someone had shot it,
It landed in a pit.

I saw a cat
Lying down on a mat,
He was next to the door,
It rolled onto the floor.

I saw the bat fly,
It was very high,
It flew into the wall,
It started to fall.

The bat was on the floor,
The cat was by the door,
The rat was in the pit,
And it was lit.

**Adam Whitehouse (10)**
**Woodseaves CE Primary School**

## AN ADVENTURE

An adventure is a fear,
As we stand so clear.
The animals in the jungle go past
As we tread on the slimy grass.
We see all the monkeys eating bananas,
When you go out into the jungle.
You'd better be careful because
You can slip on the bananas.

*Gemma Cliff (9)*
*Woodseaves CE Primary School*